Cover   *Lech Walesa addressing a Solidarity meeting.*

Frontispiece   *Many thousands of Solidarity supporters gather to celebrate Mass with Pope John Paul II during his visit to Poland.*

ESEA — CHAPTER 2
1992-93

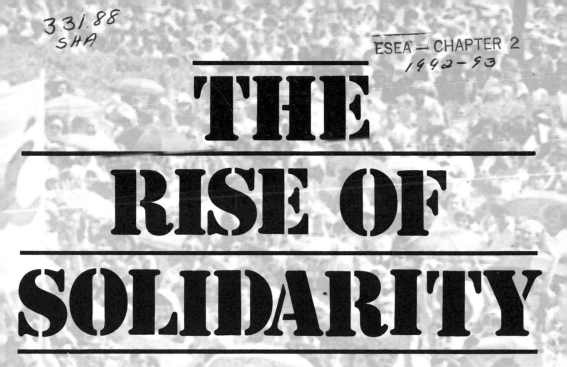

THE
RISE OF
SOLIDARITY

Tim Sharman

ROURKE ENTERPRISES, INC.
Vero Beach, Florida 32964

First published in the United States in 1987 by
Rourke Enterprises Inc P.O. Box 3328 Vero Beach, Florida
32964

First published in 1986 by Wayland (Publishers) Ltd
61 Western Road, Hove East Sussex BN3 1JD, England

© Copyright 1986 Wayland (Publishers) Ltd

Manufactured by The Bath Press, Avon, England

Library of Congress Cataloging-in-Publication Data
Sharman, Tim
   The rise of Solidarity.
   (Flashpoints)
   Bibliography: p.
   Includes index.
   Summary: Traces the post-World War II history of
Poland and discusses how and why Solidarity came to be
formed and its national and international impact.
Includes a glossary of terms and a chronology of
events.
   1. NSZZ "Solidarność" (Labor organization)—
History—Juvenile literature.   2. Trade-unions—
Poland—Political activity—History—Juvenile
literature.[1. Solidarity (Polish labor organization)
2. Labor unions.   3. Poland—History]   I. Title.
II. Series: Flashpoints.

HD8537.N783S54 1987   331.88′09438   86–20276
ISBN 0–86592–030–3

Contents

1
Occupation at Gdansk

Below *The Lenin shipyard, Gdansk, was the initial scene of unrest during August 1980.*

Opposite *By the end of August, industrial action had spread to Swinoujscie harbor.*

Klemens Gniech tried to make his voice heard above the jostling crowd that swarmed around the bulldozer he was using as a platform. For the moment he was the focus of the rapidly spreading strike. A stocky man, aged forty-two, he had been director of the Lenin Shipyard since 1976 but had himself been involved with demonstrations ten years before, when he had been a foreman. His background made him sympathetic to many of the problems that were now being shouted at him from all sides, and he appealed to the workers to go back to work while he had talks with the strike leaders. He was not unprepared for this day as rumors of industrial action had been spreading around the yard throughout the damp, restless summer.

Walesa makes a stand

He was, however, taken aback by the sudden appearance behind him of a short, slightly built man with a large moustache. Unnoticed, the man had climbed upon the bulldozer and then angrily shouted a string of accusations about his own poor treatment as a worker. That man's name was Lech Walesa, and he knew about strikes and protests.

Walesa had been a member of the 1970 strike committee. Since then, he was obsessed with the memory of the workers who had died on that occasion, shot down by police only about a hundred yards from where he now addressed the crowd. Although in and out of work for four years, having been fired from the shipyard and other jobs for his dissident activities, he was known and respected by many who were standing before him in the Lenin yard. Being one of the small group who planned this action just a week or so before, he had prepared himself for this day. Fired with righteous indignation, he had slipped away from his police watchdog and climbed the gate into the shipyard, determined to act. His action was as crucial as it was dramatic. Many were undecided until he addressed them, demanding their support for his leadership of the strike. He was greeted by waves of cheering. "I have been given the trust of the workers," he shouted at Gniech. "We are occupying the shipyard until we have got what we want. This is a sit-in strike. And I'll be the last one to leave!" As can happen in history, the moment produced the man.

A strike committee was nominated and the names read out. All nominees were approved in the euphoria of the occasion. A resigned Gniech proposed discussions starting immediately, and a large group retired to a canteen building to begin the long talks that were to mobilize the whole nation, grab headlines worldwide, cause trepidation among leaders of other eastern European countries and increase tension between the superpowers.

That was Thursday, August 14, 1980. One of the first reactions of the government in Warsaw upon hearing the news was to cut all telephone lines out of Gdansk in an attempt to contain the strikes, but to no avail. Word spread to other shipyards and factories in the neighboring cities of Sopot and Gdynia and, within days, dozens of industrial plants had stopped working. Over the weekend, the news reached Szczecin in the northwest of Poland, another major shipbuilding center, and mass meetings were called to

Gdansk, August 1980: Lech Walesa tells workers the strike must go ahead.

discuss the situation.

In the Gdansk area things moved quickly and the Inter-factory Strike Committee (MKS) was formed to coordinate demands and action. This move thwarted the plan of the authorities who hoped to negotiate factory by factory and reach local settlements. On the Monday morning a list of twenty-one demands was presented to the MKS delegates for ratification, which it duly received—the first signs of solidarity. The stage was set for a profound confrontation between government and governed. The arrival lounge of Warsaw airport filled with aluminum boxes and tripods as the world's press came to watch.

2
Poland's troubled past

By 1981 (when Walesa gave this press conference to massed reporters in Italy) there were already several versions of Solidarity's story.

History is littered with events which, at first glance, seem to be clear-cut and unambiguous but, upon investigation, defy easy analysis or even straightforward description. The significance of an event will vary from place to place, from one generation to the next. Consider the vast quantity of controversial literature still published about, say, the French Revolution or the outbreak of the two World Wars. The rise and fall of Solidarity in Poland has already become

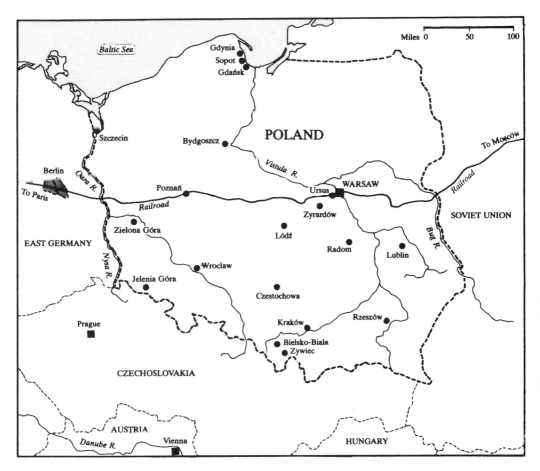

Poland today, in relation to the other countries in eastern Europe.

something of a myth, offering a kaleidoscope of meanings in accordance with the prejudice and knowledge brought to bear on the subject. It was an international media event, filmed as it happened and with thousands of witnesses. Yet what did Solidarity mean to its founders, members, sympathizers, and opponents, and why did it happen as and when it did? In attempting to investigate some of these questions, it will become apparent that there are no simple or obvious answers, although that is what many in both East and West would like to believe.

Power struggles in northern Europe
Let us look at Poland's position in Europe in relation to its history—something that Solidarity was accused of failing to do. The location of Poland on the great Northern European Plain, shoulder to shoulder with German and Russian

13

nations, is politically significant. For over a thousand years these three groups have vied for supremacy in the region, and Poland has not always been the underdog.

During the sixteenth and seventeenth centuries the Polish commonwealth was the dominant power, controlling a huge tract of eastern Europe, stretching east almost to Moscow and south virtually to the Black Sea. As recently as 1920, independent after 130 years of partition by Prussia, Austria, and Imperial Russia, Poland tried to capitalize upon the confusion that followed the Russian revolution by invading the Ukraine, gaining substantial territory before being beaten back to Warsaw by the newly formed Red Army.

There is, therefore, a turbulent history prior to Soviet domination to be taken into account when looking at this region. The Polish people set great store by history. They know the history of Poland well and are determined to retain their own version of it. For better or worse, they seem unable to forget old scores.

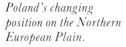

Poland's changing position on the Northern European Plain.

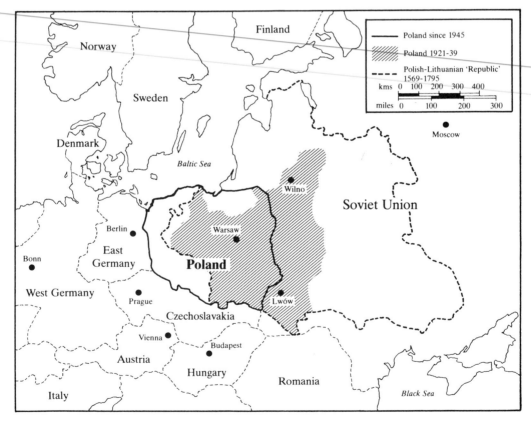

3
"Bread and Freedom"

World War II left Poland exhausted. Twenty-two percent of the population were dead and many others had fled the country. Both the eastern and western frontiers of Poland were pushed westward by the Soviet Union, whose army had broken the back of Hitler's German war machine. Thousands of families were forced to leave their cities, villages and farms to be relocated in territory previously inhabited by Germans. In the political arena, superpower mistrust

During World War II the Jews of Warsaw were rounded up and shot or sent to extermination camps.

hardened into the cold war and the Soviet Union encouraged the installation of compliant governments in its western neighbors in order to secure its frontiers against the threat presented by NATO countries.

In 1955 a military alliance known as the Warsaw Pact was formed, which included Russia, East Germany, Poland, Czechoslovakia, Bulgaria, Romania, Hungary, and Albania. (Albania withdrew in 1968.) Because the USSR is easily the largest and most powerful member of the group (much as the USA is in NATO), it can assert great political, economic, and ultimately military pressure on the other countries in the alliance. Many Poles were not against socialism but did resent having no choice in who would lead them down that path. Others sincerely believed that, as Europe settled down after the catastrophe of Nazism, Poland would develop its own distinctive and independent socialism.

Early communist rule
But, as elsewhere in eastern Europe, early leaders of the communist party (in Poland, officially the Polish United Workers' Party, or PZPR) were unnecessarily brutal and showed little administrative or economic sense. Polish recovery was slow, shortages common, and housing difficult.

The North Atlantic Treaty Organization was formed in 1949.

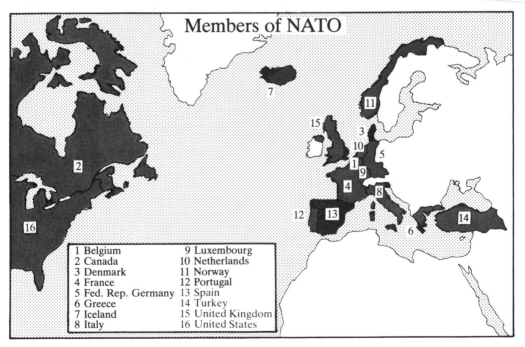

Members of NATO

1 Belgium	9 Luxembourg
2 Canada	10 Netherlands
3 Denmark	11 Norway
4 France	12 Portugal
5 Fed. Rep. Germany	13 Spain
6 Greece	14 Turkey
7 Iceland	15 United Kingdom
8 Italy	16 United States

11·LISTOPAD - 63 ROCZNICA ZRZUCENIA JARZMA ZABORCÓW

RZECZPOSPOLITEJ POLSKIEJ

ZWIĄZEK MŁODZIEŻY DEMOKRATYCZNEJ · DOLNY ŚLĄSK ·

Above *Between the World Wars, Poland experienced a brief spell of independence the people have never forgotten. This recent poster celebrates the end of partition in 1918, which the Poles regarded as a victory for nationalism.*

Left *The Soviet Union sees communism as the force that liberated Poland in 1944, as these posters in a street in Warsaw, 1982, show.*

17

Whole cities and much industry had been destroyed in the war. The working class in particular wanted to participate in factory organization. Many refused to accept authority without questioning it, having been told often enough that they lived in a workers' state. In 1956, 1970, and 1976, workers clashed on the streets with armed police, ostensibly over food price rises. In fact, their deeply felt anger and frustration resulted more from the inadequacy of a system that offered few rewards for long hours of hard work, often in poor conditions. Particularly resented were the special stores and other privileges enjoyed by party officials, police and military officers.

On Thursday, June 28, 1956, the 16,000 workers from an industrial complex in the city of Poznan marched from their workplace to the ancient town's Freedom Square behind a banner stating simply "Bread and Freedom." Denied any more democratic means of expression, they wanted their voice to be heard. A rumor spread that a delegation sent from the factory to Warsaw had been arrested. There followed two days of rioting during which Poznan city prison and police station were attacked. Special units were sent to put an end to the troubles. They did so at the expense of some seventy-five lives.

Lodz 1957: The after-effects of World War II—unemployment and food shortages—were felt most keenly by the old and poor.

This memorial to the workers who died in the Poznan riots of the 1950s, also commemorates more recent struggles.

Changes did result from the events of Poznan, however. The veteran party secretary, Wladyslaw Gomulka, dismissed during Stalin's purges of party moderates during the late forties, was recalled to the post by a reformist group, but only after a most dramatic and significant meeting of the Party Central Committee. It was attended, unannounced and uninvited, by Soviet leaders who had mobilized their troops in and around Poland. They seemed ready to intervene. After much argument, the Soviet party secretary, Khrushchev, conceded that if the Red Army engaged Polish troops, who likewise were on full alert, the fighting would be bloody and lead to years of resistance and guerrilla warfare, something at which Poles excel.

In 1980 when the Western media were insisting that Soviet military intervention was imminent, they had obviously forgotten the wise caution shown in 1956. Another misunderstanding that persists in the West is the presumption that disquiet of any kind in or among the Soviet allies indicates the rejection of socialism. In fact, most cases of protest by workers in eastern Europe have been intended to make socialism work more efficiently and in a manner closer to its theoretical principles, with particular regard to greater equality, democracy, and freedom of expression and information.

Gomulka's ideas fail

Unfortunately the high hopes invested in Gomulka came to very little. Living standards did rise, along with the rest of Europe, but at a slower rate than most countries. One popular decision he did make, however, was to end the forced collectivization of farmland, allowing peasant families to continue farming privately on their often tiny plots of land. Even today, more than seventy-five percent of agricultural land is farmed in this way. Because each farmer owns small strips of land, this system cannot produce the

Gomulka became first secretary of the Polish United Workers' Party in 1956.

abundance of food that derives from the large-scale mechanized agriculture of many other countries in both eastern and western Europe.

Investment in industry had been in huge projects, such as steelworks, which took too long to complete and rarely met production targets. In fact, the whole Polish economy was backward by most European standards, perhaps ten or fifteen years when it came to modern technology and consumer goods. In Poland, an increase in living standards meant for most people an increase in food consumption, many consumer goods being entirely unavailable. This, of course, put even more strain on the agricultural sector.

Under pressure from many economists, Gomulka introduced a policy of selective investment in an effort to concentrate on the electrical, electronic, and chemical industries, in the hope that they would prove to be export earners as well as providing goods for the domestic market. Little effort or imagination went into reorganizing agriculture, even though a key part of the new policy was the export of meat products to pay for the importation of Western technology

A large proportion of agricultural land in Poland is still owned and farmed by peasant families.

A common sight in Poland is the bare shelves in the butchers' shops. Here, customers wait in line for the last few sausages.

necessary to update industry. The end result, then, was that food was withdrawn from the home market and, once again, working people lost out. Even the chief adviser to the Planning Commission criticized these ideas, but there was no public discussion of plans and no room for public criticism. The economy limped on.

An improvement in Poland's economic situation depends on industrial exports. This factory in Poznan aims to export a third of the engines it produces.

Elsewhere in the Western world, the 1960's was a decade of rapid change and consequent unrest. The threat of nuclear genocide over the Cuban missile crisis and the appalling war in Vietnam brought the major superpowers (the USSR and the USA) into dangerously direct confrontation. These and other humanitarian issues sparked off student protests in many countries, including Poland.

In March 1968, Polish students and intellectuals demonstrated against an anti-Semitic purge, and were violently repressed by the authorities. Just a few months later the Polish people were to witness the events resulting from the growth of a more liberal interpretation of socialism in a neighboring communist country, Czechoslovakia. On August 20, Russian troops occupied Czechoslovakia and—amid fierce criticism from other parts of the world—hard line communist organization was restored there.

Overleaf *When Soviet troops occupied Prague in 1968, young Czech demonstrators waving the national flag, followed the tanks.*

Brezhnev maintained close contact with the authorities in Poland throughout the economic crises of the seventies and eighties. Here he is seen in 1982 with General Jaruzelski.

The effects of the Soviet intervention were perhaps felt most keenly by the citizens of Russia's European satellite—but supposedly independent—communist states. This was brought home by the Soviet party leader's speech, made at the Fifth Congress of the PZPR in November of that year, which was of special significance and has become known in the West as the "Brezhnev doctrine."

He asserted the right of the "socialist community as a whole" (that is, the Soviet Union and its allies) to intervene whenever "internal and external forces . . . hostile to social-ism try to turn the development" of any other communist-led country, "toward the restoration of a capitalist regime ... threatening to the socialist community as a whole."

Whether Brezhnev's advice to other Warsaw Pact members was intended as a warning or as a reassurance, words in themselves seemed unable to avert the next major crisis in Poland which followed a bad harvest in 1969. A seventeen percent increase in agricultural production was planned, but only nine percent was achieved. Meanwhile imports were growing considerably faster than exports. Industrial production was held back by a shortage of raw materials, as well as by a longstanding need for more skilled labor. There had been meat shortages for several years anyway, and now the consumer goods market was again in disarray. Trouble of some kind seemed inevitable; but the leadership, unwilling to tamper with the investment program of the five-year plan, decided to balance supply with demand by imposing a forty percent increase in the price of many foods. This was announced shortly before Christmas 1970.

The USSR is by far the most influential of the countries in the Warsaw Pact.

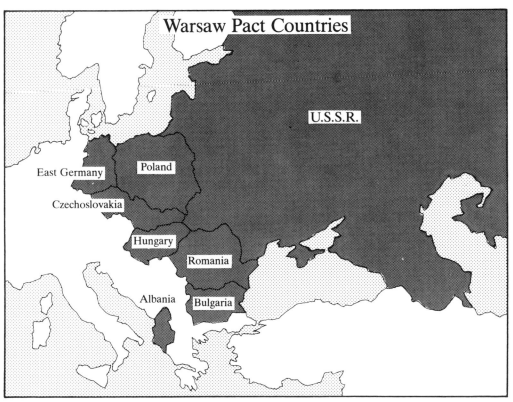

Warsaw Pact Countries

U.S.S.R.

East Germany

Poland

Czechoslovakia

Hungary

Romania

Albania

Bulgaria

4
A new party chief

In Catholic Poland, Christmas is a festival of immense importance, a time for families to congregate and spread tables with traditional niceties such as cakes and cooked meats. Had the authorities been looking for trouble, they

could not have picked a better time for their action. To the already hard-pressed Poles it was yet another sign of the insensitivity of the party, long out of touch with the mood of ordinary people.

Violence again became the order of the day. It started in the Baltic ports of Gdansk, Gdynia, and Szczecin where the authorities opened fire on a group of demonstrators. Disorder followed for many days as party buildings were burned down, and the authorities retaliated with bullets. Pressure on Gomulka increased from within the party and even from the Soviet Union, with Soviet First Secretary Brezhnev urging a political rather than military solution to the problems. Conveniently for some, Gomulka suffered

A food line in Krakow. Food shortages hit the Polish people hardest at Christmas, a time of national feasting.

a stroke and was replaced as party leader by Edward Gierek, party chief in the Silesian coal mining region. Strikes and demonstrations continued, however, into the New Year until, in February, the government was forced to cancel the program of food price rises. There are many conflicting estimates of casualties, ranging from the few dozen dead admitted by the police to the hundreds Solidarity later claimed had been killed.

Into the seventies with Gierek

By local standards, life under Gierek became a touch more liberal and past failures were openly criticized. The economy, though, did not fare so well. Seemingly full of genuine goodwill, Gierek promised to reduce party controls and to keep in closer touch with the working people. He also stressed the importance of raising living standards. For quite some time he remained popular. Sadly, though, his decade of power ended with shortages and miserable, bitter lineups for such basics as sugar, butter, meat, and even shoes. The total failure of the nation to resolve its economic problems left Poland in 1980 with foreign debts amounting to twenty-three billion dollars.

Gierek's method had been to go for rapid expansion in an effort to catch up with other European economies. But in the context of the time, and given Poland's industrial and commercial weakness, this policy was reckless. A short term boost in the demand for coal—the country's staple export—following the 1973 oil price crisis, was eclipsed by the international trade recession sparked off by the same events. And yet Poland continued to borrow money from everywhere in an attempt to buy its way into world trading circles. Consumer goods, machinery, even whole factories, were imported from the West. Between 1970 and 1975, wages rose by about sixty percent, thus increasing public demand, especially for food. From being a net exporter of food products, suddenly Poland became a net importer. The debts were supposed to be paid by exporting goods produced in the new factories, but with falling demand abroad and gross mismanagement at home (often resulting in poor quality products), neither production nor repayment targets were met. Goods that should have gone to the West for hard currency were diverted to the Soviet Union to pay for the extra oil needed to sustain the production drive.

By 1976, it was obvious that Gierek's strategy had failed,

Right *The demand for food became so acute during the seventies that livestock could not be left unguarded, for fear of theft.*

30

Students from the Technical University of Warsaw discuss ways to support workers treated unfairly.

with exports paying for only sixty percent of imports. Once again, the government panicked and, ignoring past lessons, ordered massive price increases to control demand. Once more there was a violent reaction from industrial workers and the increases were withdrawn after twenty-four hours. Alleged ringleaders were fired. So, also, was a young electrician and activist in Gdansk by the name of Lech Walesa.

As a direct reaction to the 1976 violence, a new organization was formed by sympathetic intellectuals to help victimized workers and their families. The Committee for the Defense of Workers, known by its Polish initials KOR, claimed no political aims and worked quite openly, raising money and campaigning for the release of prisoners as well as for a parliamentary inquiry into alleged police brutality. Inevitably KOR became a political force as more and more young intellectuals, impatient for change, were attracted to an organization which, in the late seventies, produced many publications expounding ideas for social, political, and economic development. Some of these ideas impressed even top party officials, but Gierek stood firmly by his program.

With the country apparently collapsing around him, Western banks hesitating to lend more money, and criticism coming from all sides, Gierek stumbled on, making grand

Far left *From 1970 to 1980 the Polish workers' banners proclaimed the same message: "we want to eat!"*

speeches and blaming economic troubles on the slump in the world market. Disappointed hopes led ordinary people to take an ever more cynical view of the party leadership. Official statistics and reports on the true state of the economy were kept so secret that even administrators in powerful positions had to rely on rumor to have any idea of what was happening. With memories of the war and all the hard times since, people began to hoard food, filling their cupboards with sugar, processed meat, or whatever became briefly available. Food prices were still absurdly low, cases even being reported of farmers feeding animals with heavily subsidized bread rather than more expensive fodder.

False propaganda of success

Referring to the seventies in an official history book published in Warsaw in 1982, Jerzy Topolski, an established journalist, wrote: "Managerial methods were not adjusted to the ambitious plans of rapidly modernizing the national economy and raising living standards. Nor was there any development of the democratic system to increase the real participation of the working people in the government of the country ... There was a growing number of arbitrary decisions concerned with investments which disregarded the

Even in the heat of industrial action, Polish strikers remember their Catholic faith.

actual possibilities and economic calculations ... At the same time the mass media continued the propaganda of success which was less and less confirmed by facts. Critical opinions voiced in the central authorities of the PZPR were being suppressed and the growing dissatisfaction in society at large was disregarded." It was damning stuff in a book designed to be read abroad.

The crunch was not long in coming. The election in November 1978 of Cardinal Wojtyla of Krakow as pope made a subtle and crucial difference to Poland. To a nation that has long sought both refuge and solace in Catholicism, the selection of a Pole as pope was an enormous boost to the people's morale. His triumphal visit to his home country in 1979 gave that extra degree of courage to the strikers in the Gdansk shipyard.

5
Walesa leads the way

So precarious was the Polish economy that a bad harvest in 1979 was enough to throw the country into a deep crisis. Faced with the need for more loans from the Western banks there had to be a cutback in imports and a redirection of all industrial output toward exporting, accentuating still

Soup and bread for sale on a market stall in a Warsaw suburb, 1981.

37

further the shortages as domestic demand far exceeded supply. When, on July 1, 1980, it was announced that meat prices were to be increased, the predictable strikes started the very next day, first at the big Ursus tractor factory near Warsaw. But this time, instead of marching and demonstrating, thus provoking police violence, the workers stayed put in their factories and elected representatives to negotiate directly with the local management for wage increases.

Managements were told by Warsaw to avoid disruption of production and make quick settlements of up to fifteen percent in the hope that the strikes would not spread. Supplies of meat were even rushed to specific factories in an attempt to "buy off" the workers. All reports of the strikes were suppressed, but KOR was well established by this time with representatives in many large plants, and the news was quickly carried throughout the country so that by the middle of July strikes were widespread. As yet there were

Despite press censorship, strikers communicated with workers in other factories by printing their own newsheets.

no demands for independent trade unions, nor were the scattered strikes coordinated by a single committee. Rushing from factory to factory, officials were therefore able to settle many disputes individually by granting wage increases and giving promises that grievances would be investigated.

The formation of Solidarity

But the unrest rumbled on, gaining momentum every day, until even the public services in Warsaw were interrupted. This was the situation when a group of activists in Gdansk decided to bring the shipyards out on strike. They demanded the reinstatement of a fifty-year-old crane driver, Anna Walentynowicz. A long-time critic of the system, she had been fired just one month before she was due to retire.

By mid-August the government was faced with a new problem. The important Baltic coast cities were united in

Surrounded by flowers and religious icons—symbols of peace and hope—Walesa spoke and listened to the people at Gdansk in August 1980.

a single strike committee (the Interfactory Strike Committee or MKS, set up on August 16), fronted by the powerful personality of Walesa and very quickly advised by leading KOR intellectuals. Most worrying was the call for independent trade unions to replace the existing ones, considered by the strikers to be tame and toothless.

Initial negotiations in Gdansk proceeded swiftly and a settlement was provisionally agreed by Walesa within a few days. However, when he took the microphone and announced to the waiting workers that an agreement had been reached, he was greeted by uproar and demands for the sit-in to continue. Reacting quickly to the mood of the crowd, he immediately reversed the decision and announced that the strike would continue. An indication of the widespread desire for change was that many strikers (even several of those who became active on the strike committees) were party members. It was also rumored that a few disillusioned factory managers urged their workers to join in the strikes.

The initial reaction of the police was to harrass or arrest KOR members. However, although hardline politicians predictably attacked the strikes, more moderate elements realized the gravity of the situation and urged discussions with strike committees. High ranking government officials were dispatched to Gdansk and the famous, much televised, and extraordinary negotiations with the newly named Solidarnosc (Solidarity) movement began.

6
The Gdansk Agreement

On August 26, 1980, the two negotiating teams, one led by Walesa, the other by Deputy Premier Jagielski, faced each other over a long, narrow table in a meeting room at the shipyard. One wall was simply a glass partition through which hundreds of workers and dozens of Western newsmen watched. The government was forced to conduct discussions of the greatest importance and sensitivity before the eyes of the world. A further extraordinary aspect of the

While negotiations went on inside the shipyard offices, crowds waited anxiously outside for the outcome.

Jagielski and Walesa signed the Gdansk Agreement on the last day of August 1980.

arrangement was that every word of the dialogue was transmitted through loudspeakers to the thousands of workers occupying the shipyard.

At first the atmosphere was warmer than many expected, but on the question of independent unions Jagielski dug in his heels. However, such was the pressure, both within the meeting room and throughout the country, that after dramatic presentations of the situation by both sides, and many telephone calls to Warsaw by Jagielski, agreements were reached and signed in a flood of publicity on August 31. The Gdansk Agreement, as it is known, took the form of comments on the twenty-one demands drawn up by the strikers on August 23. (See p. 72.) Soon afterward, the striking miners of Silesia also reached agreement, and coal mining—so essential to the economy—began again.

The Polish Parliament was called to ratify the agreements and the normally placid forum became very heated as member after member fiercely criticized the government's handling of the economy. Obviously Gierek's days were numbered. On September 5, following reports of a mild heart attack, he was replaced as first secretary of the PZPR by the fifty-three-year-old Stanislaw Kania, a long-time party bureaucrat. He made a suitably humble speech calling for socialist renewal and carefully restating Poland's allegiance to its allies in the Warsaw Pact. There was a general feeling of relief that this time some progress was being made without violence.

The Polish Parliament consists of elected representatives from regions of Poland, although most political power lies within PZPR committees.

Polish farmers wait outside a court in Warsaw to hear whether their appeal for a Rural Solidarity has been accepted.

Loyalty to the movement

Now Solidarity existed officially and opened its first office, in Gdansk, with Walesa firmly in control. Next, attention had to be turned toward the economy. The strikes had put production even further behind schedule and now time had to be spent organizing Solidarity branches and campaigning for the removal of unpopular and inefficient managers. Inevitably extremists became involved and no doubt injustices occurred; but these workers had themselves suffered injustice for years. It is fair to say that the nation was in a state of euphoric shock because the Gdansk Agreement, settled so speedily, promised so much. Mieczyslaw Rakowski, editor of the influential weekly *Polityka* and considered one of the party liberals, was quoted in an interview as saying, "There is now a deeply rooted knowledge that we must change the structure of power." Support for Solidarity exploded across the country, spreading from industrial centers to small towns and private farmers, who demanded their own Rural Solidarity. Spontaneous Solidarity cells even appeared in some schools, with children calling for pupil strikes. The enthusiastic support for Solidarity and its leader became difficult for individuals to defy without feeling socially outcast. To a detached observer, this was not without its frightening aspects.

7
Economy in chaos

Despite the agreements, though, the official registration of Solidarity did not proceed smoothly because various legal objections were raised to the wording. The intention of these delaying tactics was to get the union to recognize the "leading role of the party" in state affairs. In other words, Solidarity was being urged to remain a union and not to develop into an opposition party. Walesa's response was to threaten more strikes as he toured the country addressing workers' meetings, so eventually the registration went through without the offending clause. After so many years it was difficult for either side to change its attitude. Distrust and hostility were still felt by many workers, while the party leadership was proving incapable of finding any way of winning public confidence.

"To be beaten without surrender is a victory" reads one message in what became known as the battle of the walls.

Church leaders, like
Archbishop Glemp,
helped to combat the
hostility workers and
authorities still felt for
each other.

Although censorship was eased and more information became available, when the economic facts of life were pronounced many workers disbelieved them. They took the gloomy news to be yet another bluff to pressurize concessions from the union, which was now demanding free Saturdays at a time when every hour of labor was necessary to restore an ailing economy. Poland had not been able to repay its foreign debts before the strikes; so obviously by the autumn, after yet another bad harvest, the situation was very much worse. The production lost due to the 1980 disruptions is dramatically illustrated by the case of coal: There was a fall of sixty-two percent in the amount exported in 1980. As coal formerly accounted for over fifteen percent of all exports, the loss of these earnings was disastrous.

Finance from the West under threat

By March 1981, the government had to admit that loan repayments could not be met, which meant that no more loans would be forthcoming from Western banks. The domino effect of this was rapid and damaging. Raw material imports were cut, as were spare parts necessary to keep imported machines operating. Industrial output therefore fell even further. For example, by May, car production, was twenty-six percent below the previous year. Even shoe production was down thirteen percent, and later it almost stopped completely as the import of hides ceased. Housing

A car lottery offers ordinary people a chance to own a car, a remote prospect in Poland's present economic situation.

completions were about thirty-four percent down on 1980, making the waiting list for apartments even longer. Lacking essential supplies, some industrial plants were forced to close down and the specter of unemployment, officially non-existent in most socialist countries, reared its head.

Average monthly earnings, however, were twenty percent *above* the level of 1980, so that there was more money chasing fewer goods. Shortages and rationing inevitably followed, the black market flourished and peasant farmers saw their income from the large number of private markets increase greatly. But when they found little on which to spend their money, many withdrew to their family farms, ate their own pigs and vegetables, and traded only with friends and relatives. This situation of falling supply and rising demand spiraled on toward chaos.

Poland faced the prospect of being declared in default by its creditors, a situation that could have ended trading with all non-socialist countries. Fearing repercussions for their own economies, Poland's allies stepped in with loans, the Soviet Union alone lending over four billion dollars in the year, twenty percent of that in hard currency. The long years of Gierek's "propaganda of success" were over, and government spokesmen were openly predicting that the economy would soon have slipped back to the 1975 level. Few in the country were unaffected by the shortages and declining living standards

Censorship and the media

For Solidarity, trust in the government's intentions regarding economic and social reform was damaged further in March, when a meeting in Bydgoszcz was broken up violently by police and a Solidarity official was badly hurt. The relaxing of censorship meant that this case and any other conflict or disagreement was given coverage in the press (which people now read avidly), and on television. There was a spate of articles and programs revealing the

A Solidarity official from Bydgoszcz recovering in hospital after being viciously beaten by police.

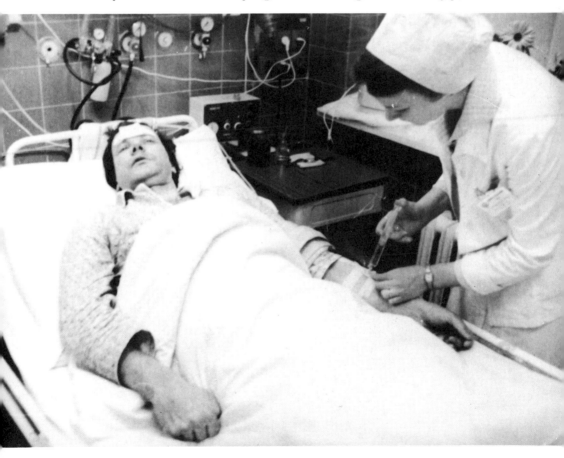

horrendous investment mistakes and corruption scandals of past years and television debates about possible ways out of the current mess.

The PZPR was deeply divided about what to do next and factions formed within it. Some pressed for more speedy economic reform with greater emphasis on the operation of market forces. They wanted central planning to be devolved to smaller, local groups, to increase flexibility.

Walesa voting at the First National Congress of Solidarity in Gdansk

Others urged a tightening of social controls and a return to a more disciplined approach to Poland's economic problems. Within Solidarity there was also some uncertainty. The great wave of optimism that swept the country when the union was formed had recruited a staggering ten million members, almost a third of the total population. A large but fledgeling organization in such circumstances could hardly hope to present a unified policy. When extremists

The Catholic Intellectuals' Club in Warsaw was a popular meeting place for Solidarity activists.

became active at local and national level, it was easy for the government to point to the genuinely anti-socialist few and claim that they represented the majority. Differences came into the open during an eighteen-day Solidarity congress held in the late summer of 1981, when it was suggested that twenty-eight percent of delegates had intellectual backgrounds. It was obvious to many sympathizers that there was a danger of theorizing activists altering the original intentions of the Solidarity movement.

Poland and the Eastern bloc

On October 16, following the Solidarity congress, the party's Central Committee met in Warsaw, and it was apparent that many speakers were on the point of despair. Party leader, Kania, expressed fears that Solidarity was becoming more and more anti-Soviet, which he, perhaps rightly, saw as a threat to Poland's interests. Around the country a total of 250,000 people were on strike for one reason or another, and the union was pressing the government with demands for referenda and other mechanisms that would have given it powers amounting to a veto over government decisions. Party officials reported that not only were thousands of members joining the independent union but a quarter of a million Poles had handed in their party cards while another 180,000 had been dismissed. Matters eased slightly when, on November 6, Solidarity called for an end to strikes that damaged the economy. However the government was still being squeezed by Western bankers who, early in December, went to Warsaw and threatened to declare Poland in default if it did not pay five hundred million dollars interest by the end of the year. The truth was that figures produced at the end of September showed only just over two hundred million dollars of hard currency and gold reserves in Poland, representing merely two weeks worth of imports.

Soviet foreign minister, Andrey Gromyko, shaking hands with Polish leader, Stanislaw Kania, at a tense meeting of the Warsaw Treaty Organization.

8
Hope and hardship

The atmosphere in Poland during that bleak autumn of 1981 was a potent mixture of ecstasy and despair as new found freedoms were explored alongside the daily grind of survival. Economically, Poland had reached its lowest point in recent history. Shortages of many goods were so acute that long lineups would form outside stores merely rumored to be expecting supplies. City centers with their dim streetlighting presented even dimmer displays in their store windows. In department stores, some floors stood almost empty while on others people waited in line for hours to pay exorbitant prices for everyday necessities, such as a bottle of shampoo. A pair of Soviet-made skis in another department could, ironically, be bought for less! A large shoe store in Warsaw featured in its window a single shoe; a high-heeled, fashionable summer shoe, hardly the thing for the broken, rain-soaked pavements outside. In small market squares, private producers haggled over the price of their eggs, sold at five times the normal store price—if the stores had any eggs at all. Much was rationed including meat, tea, sugar, sweets, butter, cooking oil, and gasoline, which did ensure that most basics were eventually obtainable. Life for city people without farming connections (or relatives in the West, to send such luxuries as coffee and soap) was very difficult and tiring. Some got up at dawn to shop before going to work only to find a long lineup already waiting. Cars were left overnight in gasline lines that stretched for miles.

The attractions of Solidarity
The places that were bustling with activity were the bookstores. The Polish have always been a well-educated and highly literate society, despite all their troubles. And now that censorship was virtually lifted, previously unavailable authors were rushed into print as quickly as paper rations allowed. Exiled poet Czeslaw Milosz had recently won the Nobel literature prize, and now he could be read by those

Opposite In Polish cities, the 1981 food shortages drove people to dig up ornamental gardens and plant vegetables.

54

prepared to wait in line. Magazines and leaflets by Solidarity and their KOR supporters were produced by the score and eagerly read. At the theater plays were performed that often contained more than a veiled hint of antagonism toward the Soviet Union.

The distinctive logo of Solidarity was everywhere—on badges proudly worn, on books, on store windows, and on walls. Every day new posters appeared outlining a new cause or demand, appealing to people's patriotism by recalling historical figures and events. Lectures were given by personalities of the day whose views—whether moderate, realistic, extreme, or fanciful—at last had an audience.

There had been genuine common ground between the government and Solidarity, and real goodwill did exist on both sides, assisted constantly by the mediating force of the Catholic Church. As late as November 1981, great hopes were raised by a series of meetings between Walesa, Archbishop Glemp, and General Jaruzelski, the long serving defense minister who had now also replaced Kania as first secretary. But on December 3, the authorities bugged a Solidarity meeting in Radom and broadcast extracts of speeches by the more extreme of those present. For those detached enough to see it, the writing was on the wall. When, on December 12, another Solidarity meeting ended with calls for a day of protest on December 17 and a referendum on the disputed matter of parliamentary elections, the government acted and its hand was revealed.

Even traditional Polish plays were open to political re-interpretation in the light of the dramatic events of the early 1980s in Poland.

National salvation?

On Sunday morning, December 13, Poles woke to find new voices on the radio and new faces on television. A man in the uniform of an army officer solemnly announced that all civilian authorities were now subordinated to a new body, the Military Council for National Salvation, which comprised twenty army officers and an admiral. Technically a "state of war" was declared by the government against its people, an extraordinary event in a modern European country. Outside, army units roamed the streets. All telephones were cut and movement about the country tightly controlled. Union and political activities were suspended and thousands of Solidarity workers arrested. Gatherings of more than three people were forbidden, except for church services, and a night curfew was imposed. It was martial law.

As soon as martial law was imposed, every street was patrolled by soldiers or tanks.

9
Martial law

There was some resistance to martial law in the form of strikes and factory sit-ins, but these were quickly, and in some cases brutally, brought to an end by units of the riot police—the much hated ZOMO. Because of a rigorous news blackout, many details of events in this period were slow to emerge and cannot easily be confirmed. The reaction

In southern Poland, mine workers occupied the coal mines in protest against martial law, but they were soon brutally evicted.

POLSKI SIERPIEŃ
1980   1981

SOLIDARNOŚĆ

in the West was a predictably righteous outcry as politicians of all inclinations felt obliged to publicly condemn the new military regime, whatever their own knowledge of the events leading up to it. More often than not, the blame for martial law was put directly upon the Soviet Union; very soon the subject became, to outsiders, simply a part of the super-power cold war game. The American government imposed sanctions on credit and trade with Poland, which brought nothing but further hardship to Polish people, affecting even the supply of chickens, fed on imported American corn.

The resistance of Catholicism

Polish journalists were carefully screened before being allowed to resume work, as were academics who, like all public employees, were forced to sign a pledge of loyalty to the regime and renounce Solidarity membership. Many refused, and ended up driving taxis or doing menial work. It was said in Warsaw that Poland had the best educated

Opposite *Only hours after the military take-over in Poland, crowds gathered outside the Polish Embassy in London to show support for Solidarity.*

Below *The United States imposed trade sanctions on the USSR because of the situation in Poland. However this caused worsening supplies and the food lines in Poland grew even longer.*

Opposite *Polish people lay flowers before the photograph of Father Popieluszko who was murdered in 1984 by the secret police.*

Below *Renowned Polish film director, Andrzej Wajda, was detained in Poland after refusing to sign a statement giving his support to measures against counter-revolution.*

taxi drivers in Europe! Cardinal Glemp wrote a letter to General Jaruzelski pointing out that these loyalty oaths would leave the government dependent upon "broken, weak and frightened people." His seemingly tough stance ensured that the Church once again became the focus of resistance to the authorities. Mass in Catholic churches was crowded each Sunday, and certain younger priests made blatantly anti-government speeches from the pulpit. Best known was Father Jerzy Popieluszko, whose murder in 1984 by secret police deeply shocked the nation and embarrassed the regime. Church property was used for a variety of meetings and performances not allowed elsewhere, and some well-known Warsaw actors appeared only at such venues, giving poetry readings and one-man shows or even mounting larger productions.

Yet General Jaruzelski insisted that "martial law does not mean putting reforms into cold storage." Some considered Jaruzelski to be both sincere and patriotic in that belief. The country had been moving inexorably toward chaos and, without a doubt, something drastic had to be done. Whether martial law and the later banning of Solidarity was the best course of action in the circumstances will be the subject of debates for many years to come. At this writing, over four years after the "state of war" was declared, it is still too early to guess.

Above *Jaruzelski was defense minister before taking over as leader of the Military Council for National Salvation.*
Opposite *The presence of armed soldiers on the streets of their towns and cities will not be easily forgotten by the Polish people.*

The Polish economy has made some progress but lacks a solid infrastructure of good roads, industrial facilities, and communications. Many of the factories and big building projects of the seventies are still unfinished. Even Polish economists estimate that standards of living will not be back to the very modest levels of 1980 until at least 1990. Investment, for example, so vitally needed to modernize outdated systems of production is down twenty-seven percent since 1980.

Poland's provincialism today

Many of the facilities of a modern industrialized state are inadequate or missing altogether from Polish life—transportation and communications being prime examples. Most main roads are narrow and pass through the centers of towns and villages. To make things worse traffic is often slowed by horse-drawn carts still widely used by Polish farmers. There is only one major four-lane road in the country and no roads of international highway standard. The telephone system is primitive, and many calls must go through an operator and be booked hours in advance. Railroads are in need of drastic reconstruction, with bridges and tracks showing signs of decay. The list of necessary improvements is long.

Nevertheless a tentative start has been made, and there are signs that a realistic assessment of the problems has

Polish army officers monitor the sale of food to ensure fair trading, and prevent bulk-buying.

been undertaken. One hopeful sign is that the draft of the 1985–89 five-year plan, although predicting only a three or four percent rise in national income, does expect investment to grow at a much faster rate than the economy as a whole. Industrial output is creeping upward again and the debts to Western banks have been rescheduled after lengthy negotiations. Some sanctions were ended after martial law was lifted in 1983 and now that the United States has withdrawn its veto, Poland can become a member of the International Monetary Fund.

Traffic is often delayed by slow-moving horse-drawn carts in Poland's cities and towns.

Over the past ten years, the production of tractors at the Ursus factory has increased considerably. Poland now exports tractors all over the world.

67

10
Solidarity today

Gdansk, 1985: Lech Walesa leads a group of former Solidarity supporters in an unsuccessful attempt to join the official May Day parade.

New state-organized unions have recruited five million members, but it is not yet certain how much power they will have and how many have joined just for the perks available. Inflation is still in double figures and may remain so for some time to come. The economic reforms promoted by Solidarity, designed to give more freedom to factory managers and a greater say to ordinary workers, have little chance of coming into operation soon, valuable as they could be in injecting vigor into the industrial scene.

Walesa's prize for peace

As for the outlawed Solidarity, Lech Walesa, after eleven months' detention and a Nobel Peace Prize, is still a nominal leader for many people, but he says little in public. Some of his colleagues still call for protests when prices rise, but these former Solidarity officials risk arrest and imprisonment when they overstep the unwritten boundary that seems to circumscribe their activities. Some have remained defiantly underground since December 1981, issuing regular statements about their continuing cause, but it is difficult to know what strength they represent—whether they are isolated individuals or part of a wider conspiracy, waiting for another opportunity to change Polish society. It is, perhaps, to be hoped that the relationship between the government and the people of Poland will be able to develop along lines of greater understanding without the additional pressures that economic deterioration inevitably brings.

The dashing of so many hopes by the imposition of martial law was a profound shock for most Poles, Solidarity supporters or not, and leaves future governments with a new

Many of those who led the Solidarity movement are still imprisoned, as this picture smuggled out of a Polish prison shows.

A military officer visiting a school in Poland to explain the reasons for martial law.

Opposite *Many Polish people resent the loss of the freedom of expression they experienced during the rise of Solidarity.*

problem. Just as the events of 1956 and 1970 have provided reason to distrust and even hate all authority, the "state of war" and all the spiritual and physical disruption it caused will long be remembered and resented by a great number of Poles. Ever since Poland lost its independence when the political map of Europe was redrawn following World War II, the country has been under the influence of its adjacent superpower, the Soviet Union. Many Polish people have found this hard to accept.

It cannot be denied that for many Polish citizens the Solidarity movement seemed to offer a chance of economic progress and a measure of political self-assertion. The demands made at Gdansk reveal both necessary and impractical aspects of Solidarity's campaign. (See page 72.) The enthusiasm and commitment the people demonstrated—coupled with the nation's valuable natural resources—are a measure of Poland's economic and cultural potential. Unfortunately, good intentions are not enough to administer a modern industrial nation, and sometimes Poland seems too entangled in its past to confront the problems of its future. To those who know Poland, its people, literature, music, and landscape, that is both a mystery and a tragedy.

Gdansk strike demands

1. Acceptance of free trade unions independent of the Polish United Workers' Party in accordance with Convention No. 07 of the International Labor Organization concerning the right to form free trade unions, which was ratified by the government of Poland.
2. A guarantee of the right to strike and of the security of strikers and those aiding them.
3. Compliance with the constitutional guarantee of freedom of speech, the press and publication, including freedom for independent publishers, and the availability of the mass media to representatives of all faiths.
4. (a) A return of former rights to: people dismissed from work after the 1970 and 1976 strikes; students expelled from school because of their views.
   (b) The release of all political prisoners. [Three were named.]
   (c) A halt to repression of the individual because of personal conviction.
5. Availability to the mass media of information about the formation of the Inter-Factory Strike Committee and publication of its demands.
6. The undertaking of actions aimed at bringing the country out of its crisis situation by the following means:
   (a) Making public complete information about the social-economic situation.
   (b) Enabling all sectors and social classes to take part in discussion of the reform program.
7. Compensation for all workers taking part in the strike for the period of the strike, with vacation pay from the Central Trade Union Council.
8. An increase in the base pay of each worker by 2,000 zlotys a month as compensation for the recent rise in prices.
9. Guaranteed automatic increases in pay on the basis of increases in prices and the decline of real income.
10. Full supply of food products for the domestic market, with exports limited to surpluses.
11. The abolition of "commercial" prices and of other sales for hard currency in special stores.
12. The selection of management personnel on the basis of qualifications, not party membership. Privileges of the secret police, regular police and party apparatus are to be eliminated by equalizing family subsidies, abolishing special stores, etc.
13. The introduction of food coupons for meat and meat products

(during the period in which control of the market situation is regained).

14. Reduction in the age of retirement for women to fifty and for men to fifty-five, or after thirty years' employment for women and thirty-five years for men, regardless of age.
15. Conformity of old-age pensions and annuities with what has actually been paid in.
16. Improvements in the working conditions of the health service to ensure full medical care for workers.
17. Assurances of a reasonable number of places in daycare centers and kindergartens for the children of working mothers.
18. Paid maternity leave for three years.
19. A decrease in the waiting period for apartments.
20. An increase in the commuter's allowance to one hundred zlotys from forty, with a supplemental benefit on separation.
21. A day of rest on Saturday. Workers in the brigade system or round-the-clock jobs are to be compensated for the loss of free Saturdays with increased leave or paid time off.

Chronology

1569–1795	Polish Lithuanian Republic (Elective Monarchy).
1905	Revolution in Russian Poland.
1918–1939	Second Republic (Independent Pact).
August 1939	Nazi-Soviet Non-Aggression Pact.
September	Germany invades Poland. Soviet Union invades Poland.
1944–1945	Liberation and Occupation of Polish lands by Soviet and Polish armies.
1945–1947	Civil war.
1948	Formation of Polish United Workers' Party (PZPR).
1949–1955	Period of full Stalinism.
June 1956	Poznan Workers' Uprising.
March 1968	Violent repression of student protests. Anti-Semitic campaign and purge.
August	Warsaw Pact forces invade Czechoslovakia.
November	Soviet leader, Brezhnev, announces to the PZPR, a socialist policy of intervention into any communist state threatened by capitalist ideology.

December 1970	Food prices rise. Bloodshed on the Baltic coast (Gdansk, Gdynia, Szczecin).
February 1971	Gierek replaces Gomulka as PZPR leader.
June 1976	Food prices rise. Violence in Radom and Ursus.
September	Formation of KOR (Workers' Defense Committee).
October 1978	Cardinal Karol Wojtyla, Archbishop of Krakow, elected Pope John Paul II.
June 1979	Pope's visit to Poland.
August 1980	Strike begins at Lenin Shipyard in Gdansk. Deputy Prime Minister Jagielski begins serious negotiations in Gdansk. Szczecin, Gdansk and Jastrzebie agreements allow formation of independent trade unions.
September	Kania replaces Gierek as PZPR leader and outlines policy of "socialist renewal." Meeting in Gdansk agrees to create an independent union called Solidarity.
November	Supreme Court registers Solidarity.
December	Warsaw Pact summit in Moscow. NATO says Warsaw Pact forces fully mobilized on Poland's frontiers.
January 1981	Lech Walesa meets Pope John Paul II in Rome.
March	Beating of three Solidarity activists begins Bydgoszcz crisis.
August	Breakdown of national negotiations between Solidarity and government.
October	General Jaruzelski replaces Stanislaw Kania as PZPR leader.
December	Warsaw Pact defense ministers meet in Moscow. Jaruzelski declares "state of war." Solidarity leaders and activists interned.
October 1982	Polish government dissolves Independent Self-Governing Trades Union Solidarity. Strike in Lenin Shipyard, ended by force.
June 1983	Pope's second visit.
July	Martial law "lifted."
December	Lech Walesa awarded Nobel Peace Prize.
October 1984	Murder of Father Jerzy Popieluszko.
Summer 1985	General Jaruzelski on his first visit to the United States declares that Solidarity no longer exists.
September	Solidarity calls for a boycott of government elections.
October	Seventy-five percent turnout claimed for government elections.

Glossary

Anti-Semitism   Persecution of Semitic peoples, especially Jews.

Cold war   In contrast with the "hot war" of 1939–45 (World War II) the cold war describes an undercover struggle involving spies, propaganda, economic aid and threats, rather than troops conventionally armed. In the second half of this century, the struggle has been between the communist and noncommunist nations.

Communism   A political philosophy taught by Marx and Lenin which argues that a revolution of the ordinary working people is inevitable to bring about a more equal redistribution of wealth. The goal of a communist state is the government of the people by all the people for the common good. It is questionable whether that has yet been achieved in any of the existing communist states.

Hard currency   Currency that is high and stable in exchange value, because it is widely accepted and constantly in demand. The American dollar is one example.

Infrastructure   The interdependent elements on which a country or organization depends. Examples are roads, communications, schools, and factories.

KOR   The Social Self-Defense Committee. A group formed in 1976 by intellectuals sympathetic to the cause of the workers and anyone treated unjustly by the state.

MKS   The Interfactory Strike Committee, formed in Gdansk in 1980 to coordinate strike plans.

NATO   (The North Atlantic Treaty Organisation). An international organization that provides cooperative military leadership and defense for its member nations. Established in 1949 with twelve nations, it now has sixteen members: Belgium, Canada, Denmark, France, Great Britain (United Kingdom), Greece, Iceland, Italy, Luxembourg, The Netherlands, Norway, Portugal, Spain, Turkey, the United States of America, and West Germany.

Nazism   Everything connected with the fascist regime of the German dictator, Adolf Hitler, and the National Socialist Party he led.

Nobel prize   An annual prize awarded since 1901 for outstanding contributions to science, medicine, literature, economics, or world peace.

Prussia   Once a German state, extending from France and the Low Countries to the Baltic Sea and Poland, it became the German Empire in 1871. In 1947 it was dissolved and divided between East and West Germany, Poland and the Soviet Union.

PZPR   The Polish United Workers' Party; the communist party in Poland, formed in 1948.

Red Army   The Russian army who seized power for the Bolsheviks during the Russian Revolution in 1917.

Rural Solidarity   The private farmers' national campaign for their own independent, self-governing union to represent agricultural needs to the government. It was registered in May 1981.

Socialism   An economic system where the community collectively owns the means of production, where production is for use rather than for profit, and where the welfare of each member of the community is of equal importance.

Superpower   An extremely powerful nation. The USSR and the USA are often referred to as superpowers.

Zloty   Polish unit of currency.

ZOMO   The riot police in Poland.

Index

Picture acknowledgments

The publishers would like to thank the following for allowing their photographs to be reproduced in this book: Associated Press 8, 22, 26, 31, 33, 42, 43, 46, 48, 49, 52, 53, 55, 59, 62, 65, 66, 70; Camera Press Ltd 12, 15, 20, 23, 24–5, 67 (bottom); 2 maj (IFL) 9, 28–9, 38, 39, 40, 56; The Photo Source 44, 68; Rex Features 19; Tim Sharman 17 (top), 21, 34, 37, 45, 57, 71; TOPHAM *frontispiece*, 11, 17 (bottom), 18, 32, 35, 36, 41, 47, 50–51, 58, 60, 61, 63, 64, 67 (top), 69; The maps on pages 13, 14, 16 and 27 were drawn by Malcolm S. Walker.